On the Pilgrim Way

to Trondheim

© TAPIR PUBLISHER, TRONDHEIM 1998
ISBN 82-519-1309-8

This book has been published with support from and in collaboration with
- The Municipality of Trondheim, the Department of Church and Cultural Affairs
- The County Municipality of Sør-Trøndelag, the Department of Business Development, Communication and Cultural Affairs
- The Directorate for Nature Management
- The Directorate for Cultural Heritage

Editor: Stein Thue
Editorial Committee: Aud Beverfjord
                                  and Leif Gaustad

Consultant: Vigdis Moe Skarstein
Translation: John C. Anthony

Graphic design: Leif Gaustad

Printed by TAPIR trykkeri

Contents

Cover photo: Detail from the gable above the Olav Portal in Nidaros Cathedral.
Photograph by Aune Forlag / Ole P. Rørvik

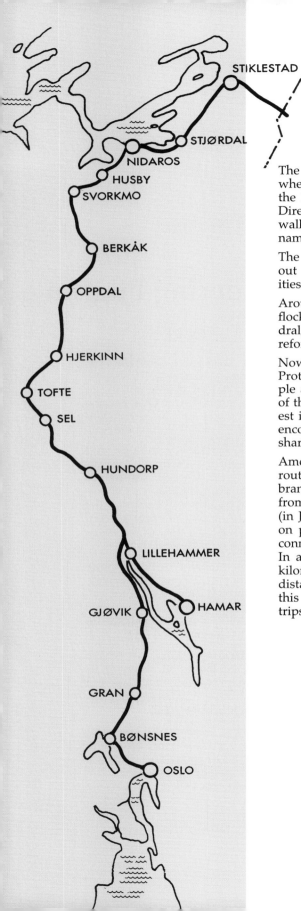

STIKLESTAD

STJØRDAL

NIDAROS

HUSBY

SVORKMO

BERKÅK

OPPDAL

HJERKINN

TOFTE

SEL

HUNDORP

LILLEHAMMER

GJØVIK   HAMAR

GRAN

BØNSNES

OSLO

The Pilgrim Way

The Pilgrim Way project was launched in 1994 when the Ministry of the Environment instructed the Directorate for Nature Management and The Directorate of Cultural Heritage to reconstruct the walk along the old roads to Nidaros (the former name of Trondheim).

The work to reopen the old roads has been carried out in close co-operation with the 29 municipalities through which the pilgrim way winds.

Around 500 ago years a steady stream of pilgrims flocked to Saint Olav's shrine in Nidaros Cathedral, from around 1050 until 1537, the time of the reformation.

Now, almost 500 years after the introduction of Protestantism saw the end of the pilgrimages, people are again encouraged to wander in the tracks of the pilgrims. The intention is to stimulate interest in an important part of Norwegian history, to encourage outdoor activities and to let people share cultural experiences.

Among the many roads leading to Nidaros, two routes have been selected for signposting: "Gudbrandsdalen" (route II on the map on page 10) from Oslo and the "Swedish path" from Skalstugan (in Jämtland) via Stiklestad (route VI on the map on page 10). The "Gudbrandsdalen path" is also connected to the road between Hamar and Fåberg. In all, the pilgrim path totals approximately 930 kilometres. It is not necessary to hike the entire distance to understand what it is all about, and this guidebook offers some suggestions for shorter trips.

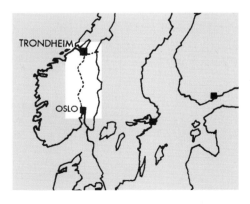

TRONDHEIM

OSLO

Pilgrim, from a miniature dating from the 1300s by Urd von Hentig.

The Wandering Pilgrim

Not long after the Saint King, Olav Haraldsson, fell in battle at Stiklestad in 1030, Nidaros became a popular goal for people seeking to redeem their souls at his shrine. Olav became Norway's patron saint, and his reputation shone far beyond the borders of his country.

Along paths and vestigial roads, through wild country and through high mountains people wended their way to Christ's Church in Nidaros, where the shrine of Olav was venerated. A substantial number of people felt the beckoning of the shrine, and pilgrimages continued there until 1537, the time of the reformation, and perhaps even beyond that.

Today we cannot pinpoint with certainty where the medieval pilgrims made their way. The trails they followed were the contemporary highways. The common road – the "people's road" – threaded along the hillsides in the valleys which had been settled first.

The road would be for walking and riding. Single-minded in its intent on reaching its destination, the road would climb up and wind down steep hills, disdaining detours around marshes or other obstacles.

In hilly terrain, traffic, weather and precipitation would cause the dissolving earth and clay to seep away, leaving a distinct furrow, a sunken road. On marshy ground the road might be paved with logs, called a *kavlebru* – a log bridge.

Pilgrims would normally travel in companies. A day's journey might stretch up to 30 kilometres for those hardy souls who could manage to hike that far. Every 8 to 10 kilometres there would be places of rest with grazing for horses. Such pastures were called "Olav's fields". Along the way there would be inns and lodgings. The oldest places for accommodation were the simple *sælehus* – houses of rest – where lodgers would have to cater for themselves. Tradition also tells us of roadside crosses, pilgrims' chapels and sacred wells along the road.

Through the centuries, the old roads have been replaced by newer ones, the soil has been tilled or the trails have become overgrown. When reviving the path, it has been necessary to consider the changes that have occurred, but the *landscape* through which the pilgrims walked remains largely the same.

The present Pilgrim Way aims to give today's wanderers an idea of what medieval pilgrims would encounter on their way to Nidaros. The path follows ancient, documented trails when these can be used. All along, the path is bound by names of places and historic monuments with links to Saint Olav's life and work.

These signposts show the way along the Pilgrim's Path.

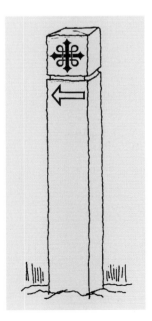

Along the way you will also see burial mounds and traces of settlements from pre-Christian times. After the pilgrimages ceased, newer historic monuments have appeared, and some of these will also interest the modern wanderer. The Pilgrim Guidebook for Trondheim describes several of these historic monuments, and they are marked on the maps. Thus the wandering will span the events of several thousand years of history.

Signposting the way for today's pilgrims, the path is marked with posts carrying the Pilgrim Way logo. These have been erected in places where the path changes direction, and at attractions mentioned in this guidebook. Signposts indicating medieval monuments and pilgrim traditions have been furnished with explanatory texts. Between these signposts smaller marking sticks will show you that you are on the right track. Most municipalities have also erected milestones which indicate the remaining distance to Trondheim and Nidaros Cathedral, the path's final destination. We hope the journey along the Pilgrim Way, or parts of it, will be enlightening and enriching, and we wish you Godspeed.

The Saint King

by Lars Roar Langslet

The major destination for pilgrimages in the Nordic countries was undoubtedly the shrine of Saint Olav in Nidaros Cathedral. The Norwegian Saint King retained his status as the "patron saint", as it were, throughout the middle ages, and was honoured just as much in neighbouring countries as in his own.

However, the impact echoed much farther away: After King Olav had been designated a saint in August 1031, the cult of Olav spread like wildfire throughout the Nordic countries, on the British Isles and in Hanseatic towns along the Baltic, finding adherents in the Netherlands, and Normandy, and even as far away as Spain, Russia and Constantinople. The oldest surviving picture of Olav was painted on a column in the Nativity Church in Bethlehem.

Olav's altar frontal from the 1300s. The motifs show at the upper left Olav's dream before the Battle of Stiklestad. At bottom left, Olav is paying a priest for masses for the souls of his opponents who are about to die in the battle. The lower right section shows Olav's death during the Battle of Stiklestad, 29 July 1030. In the upper right section Olav is declared a saint and buried on 3 August 1031. Photograph by Nidaros Domkirkes Restaureringsarbeider

This sculpture of St. Olav holding his silver axe, kept in Olav's Church in Albo, Skåne, was believed to work miracles.

Who was Saint Olav?

Olav Haraldsson was born in 995 into Harald Hårfagre's (Harald Fairhair's) family. He grew up at Ringerike in the south-eastern part of Norway, then when still in his teens he set out as a Viking, and served as an officer for noblemen in England and Normandy. He was baptised in Rouen, where he must have encountered the pious Benedictine movement. Shortly after, in 1015, he left England to claim the royal throne of Norway. On his ship he brought a number of English bishops, indicating that even at this early stage he may have seen christening Norway as his calling.

Clearly a highly intelligent man, Olav was sincere in his intentions. He was a gifted poet, and possessed great skills as a political and military strategist.

During the early years it appeared that everything went his way. He became the first national king to effectively wield his power throughout the entire country, eventually establishing an administrative network and a legal system which made it possible to hold the country together. He went on a large number of missionary excursions into those parts of Norway not yet under the sway of Christianity, especially the inland region and in the north. He provided a permanent base for the Christian faith by constructing churches and ordaining priests according to national considerations, and by introducing legal systems both for the State and the Church (the Christian law) which became a turning point in the development of the legal system: The ideals of family-based society slowly had to give way to the belief in the intrinsic value of the individual, the eminence of mercy and the duty to protect the weak.

His was least successful in creating ties of loyalty and friendship to local chieftains who felt threatened by the growing nation-wide authority of the king. This was in the heyday of Danish rule, which also saw the rule in England of the powerful Danish King Canute, who also harboured a desire to re-conquer Norway. Purchasing loyalty from Norwegian chieftains, he also fired a smouldering dissatisfaction with Olav's "harsh rule" among farmers in the inland, in Trøndelag and in the north. Resistance against Olav probably did not rise because his rule was harsher than others, but rather because he insisted on ruling. People believed that a distant King like Canute would wield his power less energetically, so that royal rule would revert to the lax affair it had always been before.

Power eroded under King Olav, and he was forced to flee. His final year on earth was spent with his brother-in-law Grand Duke Jaroslav in Kiev. This town had already grown into a spiritual centre in Eastern Europe, where theology and philosophy, monasteries and art flourished.

In 1030 he set off homeward to try to regain power. The decisive battle came at Stiklestad on 29 July. However, outnumbered and overpowered by his opponents, the King fell. His body was smuggled away, to be buried in the sandbank where Nidaros Cathedral now stands.

Soon, however, wondrous things began to take place. An eclipse of the sun was immediately linked to the battle, thought to bear tidings of the wrath of Heaven, and signifying that Stiklestad was under the shadow of Golgotha, where there was "darkness in the middle of the day". Rumours of the King's sudden healings were rampant. One of these concerned one of the men who slayed the King, Tore Hund, whose wounded hand was healed after a drop of the King's blood fell on it, causing him to break with his ways and set off on a pilgrimage of atonement to Jerusalem.

The body was exhumed more than a year after the death of the King, and the Bishop, supported by the masses, declared him a holy man. Canonisation was then a matter for the local Church, but the sanctity of Olav was nevertheless fully approved by the Pope in Rome.

Olav sculpture from Brunlanes in Vestfold. Photo by Karl Teigen

Olav was sanctified as a martyr. His death under the sign of the cross was seen as indisputable proof that God had used him as his instrument. His sanctification was thus not affirmation of his behaviour after an uncommonly pious life. He was moreover honoured as Norway's apostle, because he completed the long and arduous process of christening Norway.

The combination of martyr and apostle is unique, and perhaps constitutes the most important reason why the cult of Olav grew so strong and reached so far.

The Battle of Stiklestad must have appeared as the definitive downfall of a failed king. However, the tables were turned: The two main objectives Olav had been fighting for, uniting and christening Norway, gained their final victory through his death as a martyr. It is safe to say that the death of no other man has had such major impact on the history of Norway.

Olav became a saint deeply loved by the people because he appealed to more or less all groups. He was the champion of peasants and sailors, the patron saint of travelling merchants and city dwellers, defender of the monarchy and the protector of the needy. He was a hero after the fashion of the times, a knight of the faith as if springing from the imagery of the stories of the knights.

The legends of the saint king offered very many exciting and colourful events that seemed to only grow with each passing generation. Many Nordic sculptures and paintings of Saint Olav have been retained from the middle ages, some of them the most exquisite pieces of art from this epoch. There is also a rich tradition of folk tales and songs about him. A typical expression of his popularity is that the name Olav became one of the most commonly used in all the Nordic countries, and it lives on in the name of several flowers.

Through centuries St. Olav remained the national symbol of the realm of Norway, the "eternal King of the Realm" (rex perpetuus), and "St. Olav's Act" had the status of being the very foundation of justice and fairness. Kings regularly referred to Olav in their decrees and letters, far into the period of the union with Denmark.

But the symbols themselves remain: The axe held by the lion in our national coat-of-arms is the martyr axe of Saint Olav. In the national anthem, Bjørnstjerne Bjørnson has included Olav's kingly deeds which have left their mark on Norway ever since: "Olav painted the cross on this country with his blood".

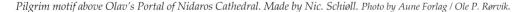

Pilgrim motif above Olav's Portal of Nidaros Cathedral. Made by Nic. Schiøll. Photo by Aune Forlag / Ole P. Rørvik.

At Sea and on Land

by Arnulf Selnes

Flocks of pilgrims wandered the medieval roads leading to Nidaros (the former name of Trondheim). Some would seek Saint Olav's shrine hoping to find a cure for their physical ailments, others to find salvation for their souls. Some would be hoping to pay penance for their misdeeds, and others might have been spurred by wanderlust or the hope of adventure. All in all there might have been a few thousand each year, a large number of people in those days, at a time when Nidaros only had two or three thousand inhabitants. Most pilgrims would probably follow the main road from the south across the Dovre plateau down the Orkla Valley to Svorkmo, then across the hills to Skaun, 35 kilometres from Nidaros.

Seasoned travellers would consider 35 kilometres to be a full day's journey, and this would be divided into four stretches of around nine kilometres, each called a *rost*, at the end of which there would be a place to rest and to let the horses graze. Pilgrims and other slow travellers would hardly manage more than two "rosts" a day, which would be called "short" day journeys. Hence there would most likely be an inn every second "rost", at least along the main thoroughfare.

From Skaun the road passed Buvika and Halsbrekka to Øysand. From the ferry landing at the mouth of the Gaula river it continued across Gaularåsen, which these days is called Byåsen, to Nidaros. On their final day of travel before reaching their destination, the pilgrims liked to give themselves ample time and probably only travelled one "rost". Thus they would be ensured enough time for a rest at Feginsbrekka, the Hill of Joy, where they would get the very first glimpse of their destination. Similar lookout points (mons gaudii in Latin) are also found outside Prague, Jerusalem and Santiago de Compostella (mont gozo in Galician). The two last resting places before Nidaros, both probably with inns or shelters, probably lay at the Gaula ferry landing and in the Kystad/Vådan area of Byåsen.

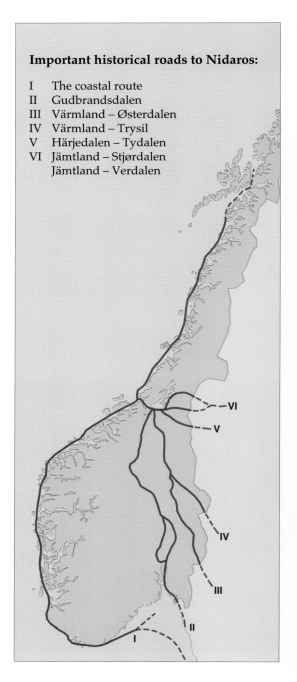

Important historical roads to Nidaros:

I   The coastal route
II   Gudbrandsdalen
III Värmland – Østerdalen
IV   Värmland – Trysil
V   Härjedalen – Tydalen
VI   Jämtland – Stjørdalen
     Jämtland – Verdalen

*St Michael and the defeated
dragon. Found at Vassfjellet.
Photo by the Science Museum*

Roads led from "Østerdalene" – the Eastern valleys – which would probably be more suitable for those pilgrims wishing to plod through the wilderness in solitary hardship, being lifted nearer the heavens across the mountains. The final stages of their journey would take them across Vassfjellet mountain. Up there, by Evenstjønna (a small lake), with its holy waters and the Chapel of St. Even, the view would open on to Nidaros far to the north. The path would lead by Rosten, indicating one "rost" to go through Byåsen further north into town. Many pilgrims came through Sweden and countries further east. The holiest path for them to choose would be the one the Saint King himself had followed on his way through Jämtland down the valley of Verdalen to Stiklestad. From there, the road would lead via Lånke to Nidaros.

The links across the water to the countries by the North Sea were strong. Thus some pilgrims came by ship to Nidaros, from Ireland and England, from the Isle of Man and Scotland, and from the wide reaches of *Norgesveldet*, the Norwegian domain, which included the isles of *Vesterhavet* (the Western Sea), the Faeroe Islands, Iceland and Greenland.

Around 1075 the learned scholar Adam of Bremen wrote:

"The Norwegians' capital is *civitas Trondemnis*, the city of Trondheim, which is now adorned with churches and visited by a great many people. In this city rests the body of the very holy King and Martyr Olav. At his grave, the Lord even today works wondrous miracles, so that the many who hope to be helped by the good deed of this holy martyr flock there *a longinquis regionibus*, from distant lands. From Ålborg or Vendsyssel in Denmark, where they embark, it is a day's voyage across the sea to Vik, a town in Norway (probably Tønsberg). From there the voyage continues to the left along the coast of Norway, on the fifth day ending in Trondemnis itself. There is another road too, from the Danish province of Skåne, across land all the way to Trondemnis, but the journey goes not as fast in the mountains, and travellers shy from taking this road, as it abounds in danger."

The voyage from the Oslo fjord to Nidaros would probably take a month rather than five days. Extended sea voyages were also demanding and unpredictable, with long waits for favourable winds. Thus sea voyages were for freight rather than for travel. When going far, people would often go by road when possible, so there was steady traffic along the highways. Even royalty travelled by road, at least when on pilgrimages, and even more so when doing penance.

Map of the Pilgrim Way to Trondheim

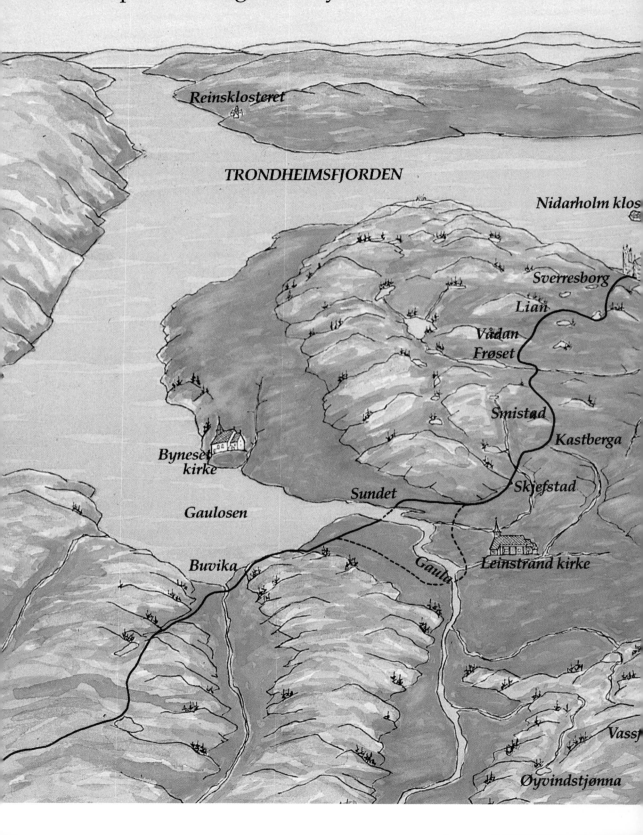

Reinsklosteret

TRONDHEIMSFJORDEN

Nidarholm klos

Sverresborg

Lian

Vådan
Frøset

Smistad

Kastberga

Byneset
kirke

Skjefstad

Sundet

Gaulosen

Leinstrand kirke

Buvika

Gaula

Vass

Øyvindstjønna

In the middle ages, there were churches at Byneset, Bratsberg, Klæbu, Leinstrand and Tiller. Here we see the churches as they stand today. Medieval churches in the city itself are depicted in the model of the city on page 31.

Drawing: Børge Engberg

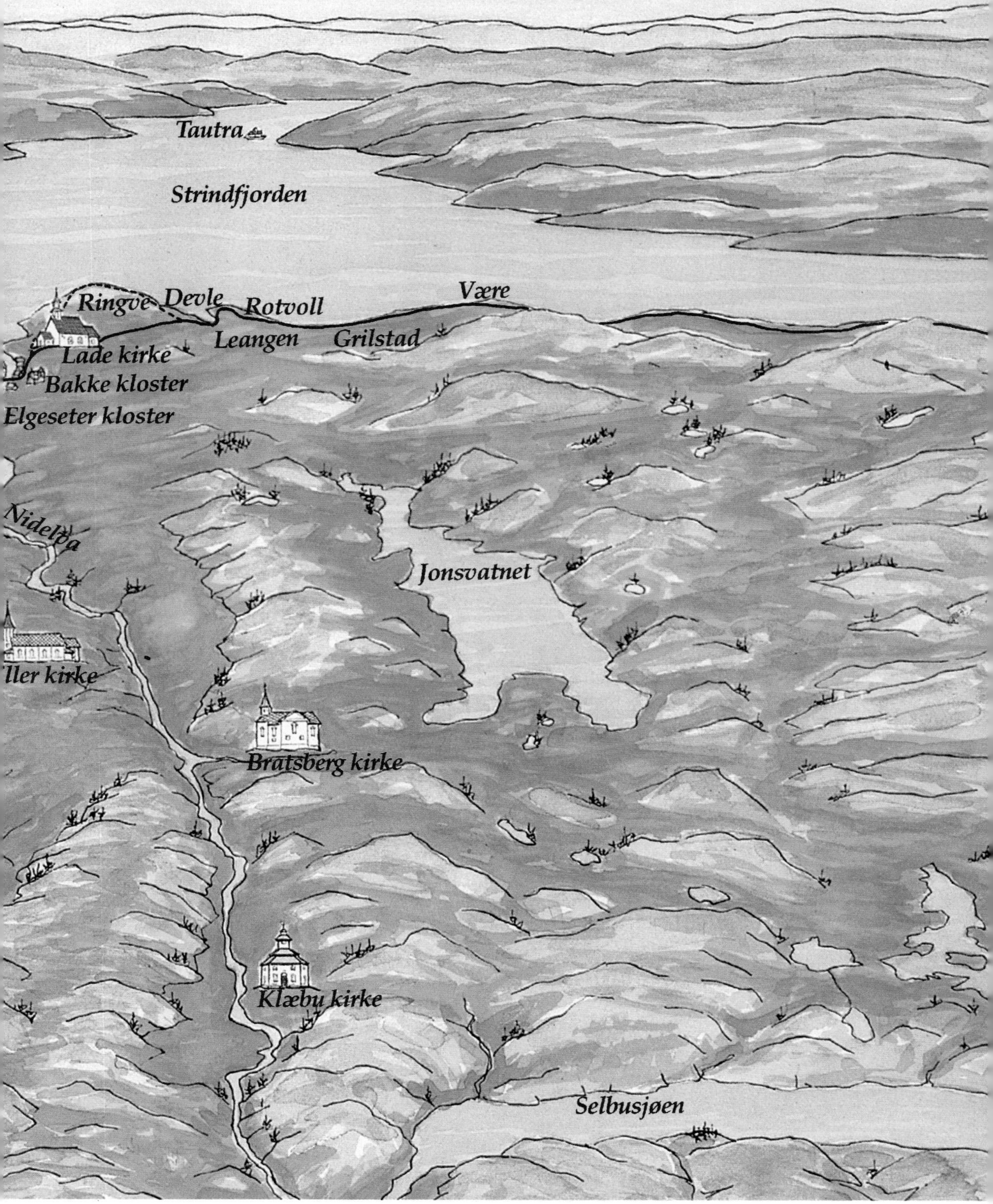

Tautra

Strindfjorden

Ringve Devle Rotvoll Være

Leangen Grilstad

Lade kirke

Bakke kloster

Elgeseter kloster

Nidelva

Jonsvatnet

Iler kirke

Bratsberg kirke

Klæbu kirke

Selbusjøen

On the Pilgrim Way: From Sundet to Nidaros

by Arnulf Selnes

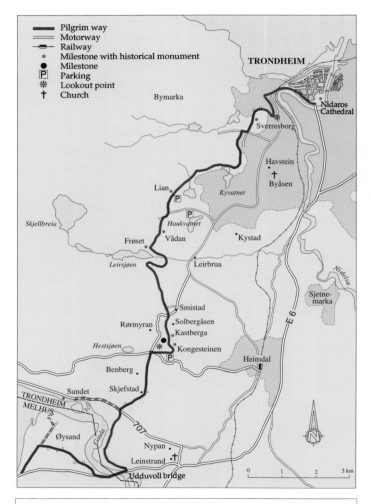

The distance from Sundet to Nidaros Cathedral is approximately 20 kilometres. Sundet is reached by following National Road 707 close to four kilometres from Klett in the direction of Byneset.

Kastberga (the hill where one threw sticks and stones to announce their passage) by Hestsjøen is reached by following the Pilgrim Path from Sundet via Skjefstad, or the Ringvål road from Heimdal, or the Smistad road from Leirbrua at Byåsen. The place to take off from the Ringvål road is signposted, two hundred meters from the Fjøsvollan junction with the Smistad road.

Sundet

Around AD 1700 the main highway from the south was re-routed from Orkladalen (Orkla valley) to Gauldalen (Gaul valley). However, the road via Skaun continued to be the king's highway from western Norway.

Up until 1859, Sundet by the mouth of the Gaula river was a traffic junction with a pier for ships and a ferry landing, an inn and a marketplace.

From Sundet up the hills past Skjefstad the path follows the highway constructed by Road-Master General Krogh starting in 1788.

Traces of the original riding path also lead from the area below Skjefstad.

The name of this farm may stem from *skipstad* – ship's place, literally – and may be a reminder of an older ferry landing which might have been obliterated by a landslide.

Shorter pilgrimages

- **Kastberga – Lian** (6.8 km). The place to take off from the Ringvål road is signposted two hundred meters east of the Smistad cross-roads. Follow signs saying "Sivilforsvaret" (Civil Defence).
- **Lian – Nidaros Cathedral** (7.8 km). The tramline (Graakallbanen) goes from St. Olav's gate to Lian everyday. From Lian, follow Lianveien and Gamle Lianvei to Kyvatnet. From there follow Antonie Løchens vei, Dalhaugveien, Torshaugveien, Lagmann Lindboes vei and Fjellseterveien to Sverresborg.
- **Sverresborg – Nidaros Cathedral** (4.2 km). The path from Sverresborg to Nidaros Cathedral is marked on the map of Trondheim on p. 42.

The ferry landing Sundet. Photo Ola Storhaugen

The ferryman. Figure carved in wood. From Sundet farm. Photo Ola Storhaugen

Hollow road by Kastberga. Photo Bjørn Sæther

Kongesteinen – The Kings' Stone

Around AD 1700 the highway from the south led via Gauldalen and in to the old trail under Kastberga. The cross-roads developed into a busy marketplace. At the same time the road was improved so that wagons could use it. Parts of the old riding path can be seen along the carriageway as soon as we start walking along Kastveien. Traffic, weather and precipitation have eroded the road so it became more of a sunken hollow. The narrow V-shape bears witness to this being a riding path. Just beyond, in the carriageway, the smooth rock of the Kings' Stone rises into the road, two meters across. According to ancient custom, the Kings' Stone was adorned with branches of juniper and spruce on each 23 June, which is the day for the Midsummer Eve festival. Legend has it that three kings are buried underneath this "stone", which probably is part of the bedrock itself.

Kastberga

From Kastberga we can see Rørmyra, Øyberget and Halsbrekka to the south-west. Due south lies the Gauldalen valley. Behind us by Kastveien lies the abandoned cotter's farm Kastet. The name of this farm reveals a pre-Christian superstition in trolls and goblins and supernatural powers, a belief which was strong in the middle ages and lasted well into the 1700s. When difficult sections of road were encountered, it was necessary to warn goblins by throwing a stick or a stone – hence *Kastberga*, literally throwing rocks – as a surprised and cantankerous goblin who could not manage to slip away in time might cause a horse to rear or stumble. Pilgrims would ride or walk this way, indeed King Christian V rode this way on his royal visit in 1685. Along the road you can see where gravel and stone for the carriage way have been dug out. Kastveien was the main road from the south to Trondheim up to 1772, and remained the highway connecting to the western part of Norway until 1788. The last section of the road to Smistad follows an abandoned part of Krogh's road which replaced Kastveien in 1788.

Toward the lake of Leirsjøen

From Smistad pilgrims would probably walk via Kystad to Nidaros, but the present path follows another old road by Leirsjøen and down Vestmarka. Prior to the damming of Leirsjøen in 1800, the road crossed by the old ford where the river runs from the lake, just above the islet in the lake.

Frøset

The old Frøset farm by Leirsjøen is now abandoned, but the buildings are kept in repair. It has been suggested that during pre-Christian times Frøset may have been a place of cult worship for Frøy, the Norse god of fertility. Typical of these places honouring Frøy is that they lie along deserted stretches of old road.

Vådan

Vådan (the name derives from old Norse *viðr*, which means wood) was a cross-roads in pre-Christian times. A side road from Skaun crossed the fjord from Børsa to Steinshylla by Byneset Church, continuing through Bergskaret along Skjelbreia via Vådan to Kystad. Along the road from Vådan toward Kystad one can see a number of burial mounds from the Iron Age. From Vådan there was a riding path via Solem and Lian down Vestmarka, approximately following the present *Gamle Lianvei* (the Old Lian road) from 1846. We shall follow this.

Boundary stones

During the period when Norway was ruled by Denmark, royalty and noblemen were received by town notaries and dignitaries at the town boundary stone at Dalhaug. The boundary stone indicated the town tax boundary, as well as the boundary to the former municipality of Strinda, the area south and west of the town, and to Bymarka. Sadly the stone disappeared in the 1950s. For the rest of the distance to Sverresborg (Sverre's Castle), the road constituted the boundary between Bymarka and Strinda. The entire area from Nidelven up to here belonged to the Strinda farms called Havstein and Stavne. In the garden of Torshaugveien no. 5, the boundary stone from 1788 of Catharina Meincke Lysholm, Agent of the Royal Court, still stands, indicating the boundary line between her property Havstein and the neighbouring farm of Stavne Øvre. Other than a few cotters' farms in the area, there were no houses here prior to 1800, and the area was densely forested during the middle ages. Torshaug in Bymarka was the mountain dairy farm for Kystad.

In a marshy section the road was often constructed by piling earth to raise the level of the terrain – an earthen bridge.
Photo Aud Beverfjord

Wet sections of the road might be paved with logs. Drawing: Aud Beverfjord

Sverresborg at the time of King Sverre as reconstructed in the drawing by Gerhard Fischer, architect

Sverresborg (Sverre's Castle)

Protected by a circular wall at the top of Steinberget lay Sverresborg, the citadel built by King Sverre in 1182. Stones for the construction were taken from the quarry under Marienberg, by the road at Nidarli. King Sverre called it mount Zion. Having studied to become a priest, he was well aware that Jerusalem, the Zion of the Bible, was guarded against the west and against the Day of Judgement by the mount Zion found there. Sverre was also familiar with the ties between the legends of Olav and the Book of Psalms, 48, 2–3: "Great is the Lord, and greatly to be praised in the city of our God, in the mountain of his holiness. Beautiful for situation, the joy of the whole earth, is mount Zion, on the sides of the north, the city of the great King."

Tavern

Around Sverresborg lies Trøndelag Folkemuseum with its old houses and collections, well worth a visit. Situated by Sverresborg allé, the inn called *Tavern* was moved here from the dock area at Brattøra in 1950. During the 1700s and 1800s, Tavern was the ferryman's inn by the mouth of Nidelven. *Tavern* remains a place to drop by for refreshments, just as the medieval *tafernishús* – tavern houses – were inns for pilgrims and other wayfarers.

Feginsbrekka

From Sverresborg the road emerged on the hillside of Nidarli. Close to present-day Sverdrups road is the probable site of Feginsbrekka – the Hill of Joy – where pilgrims would stop to rejoice in the view, fall on their knees to pray and praise the Lord. A splendid view opened on the town and Christ's Church. In Sigrid Undset's book "The Mistress of Husaby", Kristin Lavransdatter experiences her encounter with Nidaros:

"Kristin stood on Feginsbrekka and saw the city lying below her in the golden sunlight. Beyond the river's broad shining curves lay brown houses with green turfed roofs, dark domes of leaves in the gardens, light-hued stone houses with pointed gables, churches that heaved up black shingled backs, and churches with dully gleaming leaden roofs. But above the green land, above the fair city, rose Christ's Church, so mighty, so gloriously shining, 'twas as if all things else lay prostrate at its feet."[1]

We do not know exactly where Feginsbrekka was, but a similar view of present day Trondheim can be enjoyed by taking the little detour to Utsikten (the view).

1 From the translation by Charles Archer of Sigrid Undset: The Mistress of Husaby, Bantam 1978, ISBN 0-533-11030-6.

Ilevollene, Hospitalet and Kalvskinnet

Below Feginsbrekka and the slopes carpeted with lush forests lay the bare Ilevollene (Ile fields), probably grazing land, but more familiar as the battleground where King Sverre and King Magnus Erlingsson fought in 1182. Access to the town across the isthmus of Nidareid was controlled by a wooden fortification with palisades and a moat, constructed by Archbishop Øystein Erlendsson during the winter of 1177–78. A distance away from the town was the Hospital, the "*Spital*" in Vollene (the fields). Here the town's poor and sick were cared for, but it also served as a hostel for wayfarers and pilgrims. The medieval town started at Munkegata. Adjacent to the town was the "field", later called Kalvskinnet (the calf's skin). The name is said to derive from the fact that the tenant farmer holding this field was required to pay a calf's skin to the owner for the use of the land.

Olavskilden (Olav's spring)

At Marinen, close to Elgeseter bridge, lies *Hadrians plass*, named after Pope Hadrian IV (1154–59), better known as Cardinal Nicolaus Brekespeare. In 1152/1153 he established the Archbishopric of Nidaros, as the representative of the Pope. Olavskilden, Olav's spring, is found at Hadrian's place, hidden under a tall earth embankment. Olavsbrønnen, Olav's well, however, lies inside Nidaros Cathedral itself. The saga relates how the high altar in Christ's Church lies over the very place in the river bank where Olav's body had been buried. Others claim that the burial site was beside the almost forgotten Olav's well.

Hadrian's place where Olavskilden lies in the earth embankment behind the fountain
Drawing:
Kari Støren Binns

On the Pilgrim Way: From Saksvikkorsen to Nidaros
by Aud Beverfjord

The Pilgrim's Way from the north winds from Skalstugan in Jämtland via Sul and Stiklestad to Nidaros (the former name of Trondheim). The major part of pilgrim traffic from the north and east passed through Stiklestad, the battleground where Olav Haraldsson fell. From Verdal the road went by Levanger and Stjørdal to Malvik. By Follsjøen (lake) in Mostadmarka in Malvik it is said a chapel frequented by pilgrims was situated there during medieval times. Sources suggest that the high road from Mostadmarka to Trondheim passed via Jonsvatnet and Bratsberg and into the town by Elgeseter bridge. However, from Follsjøen we choose *Kjerkstien* – the Church path – by Bakken in Malvik, passing the boundaries between the municipalities of Malvik and Trondheim at Saksvikkorsen.

The section of the Pilgrim's Way we follow from here on does not trace any medieval path. However, it follows a trail which offers modern travellers a landscape abounding in historical monuments.

The name of Saksvikkorsen has ancient roots. It reflects a historical person, in the Royal Sagas of Snorre spoken of as *Saksi á Vík* – Saksi from Vik. The farm called Vik must have been close to the place now called Saksvikkorsen, where today you will find a milestone stating that the distance to Nidaros Cathedral is 14 kilometres. West of this junction is a mound in the terrain, a burial site from the Iron Age.

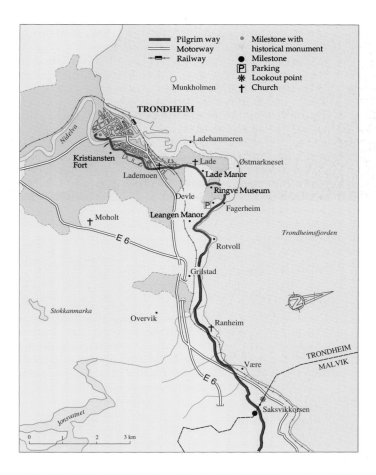

Shorter pilgrim hikes

- **Saksvikkorsen – Ringve Museum (9.8 km)**. The path goes along Bostadveien and Ranheimsveien to Nordliveien at Nedre Charlottenlund (just before the railway underpass). Follow Nordliveien and Sjøveien to Rotvoll Nedre. From there, the road follows the nature path along the fjord to Fagerheimsbukta. The Trondheim map (page 42) shows how to proceed via Smedstuveien and Olav Engelbrektssons allé to Ringve Museum.

- **Ringve Museum – Nidaros Cathedral** (4.6 km, omitting the detour). A recommended detour is to follow part of *Jarlestien* (The Earl's Path), the natural path from Ringvebukta around Østmarkneset to Korsvika. From there one can walk from Korsvik allé to Lade Church, then follow the path marked on the Trondheim map.

Today, the burial mound is partly hidden by bushes, but when it was built, some time during the middle ages, it enjoyed a strategic location, being highly visible – especially from the sea. Following the Pilgrim Way into Trondheim, we can take a break here to enjoy the view of the Trondheim fjord and the Lade peninsula.

The view from Saksvik-korsen of the Trondheim fjord with the Lade peninsula in the background.
Photo Svenn Erik Lyngstad

Above the old E 6 (European highway no. 6) we pass the Være farms. The path follows Ranheimsveien to Charlottenlund, first through Være and then Ranheim – these being farm names dating from the early Iron Age. On this stretch we pass more burial mounds. By the Vik river a bridge foundation, possibly from the middle ages, has been discovered.

This is the landscape in which the farm called *Vik* probably was situated during the older Iron Age. Testifying to this fact are the neighbouring farms of Nervik and Overvik (Lower Vik and Upper Vik). Overvik was also called *Nygården* (New Farm), thus possibly being the original Vik farm which has been moved further up from the sea. Vik river, running here, is named after the farm. The original Vik farm must have been lying on the west bank of the river, and Vik river may have been the farm boundary to the east.

At the farm of Presthus, which has been separated from Vik, we find two stone monuments from pre-Christian times. They have probably stood by a path leading between the farms, from Lade to Saksvik, and possibly even further east. Gerhard Schøning (1722–1780 – headmaster at the Cathedral school and historian) claimed that a medieval church stood here, but this is disputed. During medieval times Nedre Vik (Lower Vik), Øvre Vik (Overvik) and Presthus, previously called "Nedre Vig", were first monastery property under the Bakke Monastery, and later belonged to Elgeseter Monastery. In this historic landscape we also find the Grilstad farm, whose name is not found any other place. The first syllable of this name probably derives from an ancient name of the

river passing the farm. Just to the east of the buildings we can see a burial ground which also ties the farm to the Iron Age.

We then wander on past Ranheim School, passing Ranheim Church, continuing toward Charlottenlund. At this place, just before the railway underpass, the path turns off, passing through the residential area in Nordliveien, which we follow to Sjøveien. Following Stuttveien, we then turn right toward the sea, where we may follow *Jarlestien*, a path constructed to take people around Østmarkneset (the Østmark promontory) to Korsvika. Here you will find on the left Trondheim Teachers' College, housed at Rotvoll Farm. Archaeological excavations have proved that there was agriculture here as early as the Bronze Age, and the name itself ("Rot"/root) indicates that this land was cleared of tree stumps.

Following the path around the promontory at Rotvoll, we pass Statoil's Research Centre and arrive at the Bay of Leangen with Leangen Manor on the slope to the right. The manor was built in 1820–21, along with the English landscaped garden. The name *Leangen* means "bay of clay" – and the manor lies by a shallow bay filled with clay. Leksvik and Frosta are visible on the other side of the fjord. The island of Tautra with its characteristic profile is also visible in the fjord, with the ruins of the Cistercian monastery, founded by monks from Lyse Monastery near Bergen in 1207. No longer independent in 1532, it was placed under the Crown in 1537.

Leangen Manor, was built in 1820. Today this manor is used by the Municipality of Trondheim for official representation and as a course centre. © T. Moen

The path continues alongside the sea to Smedstua, then follows Smedstuveien. It is possible to follow Jarlestien around the Østmark headland, via Korsvika to Lade Church. The path winds along Smedstuveien through a residential area and a bit longer along Olav Engelbrektssons allé. From this lane we turn left entering the Botanical Gardens at Ringve. Ringve Museum is originally a manor, once owned by Alderman Jan Wessel, father of Peter Wessel Tordenskjold – the Norwegian naval hero. In the 1950s Russian-born Victoria Backhe initiated the creation of a museum of musical history at Ringve. The barn has been rebuilt into a concert hall. In the main building there is a valuable collection of old musical instruments.

From Ringve we follow Lade allé to Lade Manor. During the saga period, Ringve was probably part of Lade, with the same owner up to 1661. Devle, another farm situated northeast of Ringve, was probably originally part of Lade. The name derives from the Norse *hlað*, meaning "place of storage". It may have been a place where goods were stored in ancient times, and also a place from where goods were shipped. Snorre relates how Harald Hårfagre (Harald Fairhair) owned a large farm here. This was probably an older farm which he made into the Royal residence. In ancient times Lade was the seat of pre-Christian cult worshippers. Olav Tryggvasson challenged the powerful Trønder chieftains by burning their place of worship. We do not know exactly where this stood. Saint Olav made Lade crown land, and it was later placed under the administration of Bakke Monastery. The magnificent manor seen today was built by

Lade Church. The oldest part of the church is probably from around 1180.

Lade Manor. A Chief's Manor from the time of the Vikings. Present buildings were constructed in 1811. Drawing by Svein T. Rasmussen

Ringve Museum. The only museum of musical instruments in Norway.
The buildings were constructed during the second half of the 1800s. Photo by Stein Thue

the prosperous merchant Hilmar Meincke in 1811. From the manor an alley leads down to medieval Lade Church, the oldest part being from around 1200.

Continuing on the way to Nidaros Cathedral, we follow Jarleveien, Ladeveien, Mellomveien, Grundtvigs gate, Lademoen allé and Arne Bugges gate. This area bears the name Lademoen. According to Gerhard Schøning, this a "large, beautiful and level area". When he saw this landscape, during the second half of the 1700s, it was overgrown with heather and bushes, but evidently had been cultivated in former times. According to Schøning, there were also several "Giant Mounds", burial mounds built of sand and stone.

The path then passes Lademoen School, crossing Innherredsveien. We continue along Stad-singeniør Dahls gate to Weidemanns vei, which we follow up to Småbergan (the little knolls) by Kristiansten fort. The fort was built in 1681–84 according to plans drawn up by General Johan Caspar de Cicignon. From here we can see Munkholmen – Monk Island – in the fjord. In ancient times this was the place of executions, and here the head of Kark the slave was placed on a stake in 995 after he had killed his master Earl Håkon, the last pagan chieftain in Trøndelag, as we can read in Snorre, Olav Trggvassons Saga. During the Middle Ages, a more peaceful atmosphere permeated the island, as Nidarholm monastery was founded here at the beginning of the 1100s by Benedictine monks. It was dedicated to St Laurentius, saint of the sick and poor. The monastery was closed after the Reformation in 1537.

We then follow Kristianstens gate, Kristianstensbakken and cross Nidelva river across the Old Town Bridge. We then turn left, leaving the network of roads, and follow the path down to Marinen by Hadrians plass, where we meet the path which comes from the south.

The Medieval Landscape

by Bjørn Sæther

We perceive the natural landscape as eternal and never changing, even if we can see signs of change almost daily. Mountains, valleys, lakes, beaches and oceans are there from when we were born until we die. Nonetheless, nature and her seasons and man change the character of the landscape.

Pilgrims coming down the Orkla valley or via Hølonda would have to cross the Gaula river to start the final lap to their destination. During the height of the pilgrimages, in 1345, Norway's worst natural catastrophe, in terms of the loss of human lives, occurred here. There was a landslide between what is now Hage bridge and Hovin, damming the Gaula river to a height of 30 m above its normal level. When after some days the water had managed to work its way through the dam, something like 150 million cubic meters of clay and gravel thundered down the valley and into the sea.

Among the plants bearing Olav's name we find one-flowered winter-green (moneses uniflora), a modest but beautiful little flower in the spruce forest (in Norwegian called "olavsstake"). Photo Roar Hjelmstad

The Icelandic Skålholt Annals relate how 250 people perished, and that the number of poor people and wayfarers who died probably was no less than those who could be counted. Some of these wayfarers may have been on their way to or from the shrine of Saint Olav in Nidaros. The annals further relate how the valley remained impassable for several years. Gaulosen, the mouth of the Gaula river, was probably filled up and moved quite a ways in 1345. Later clay landslides have also made the road to Nidaros (the former name of Trondheim) difficult.

When the pilgrimages to Nidaros started, pilgrims saw another forest landscape than we do today. Where now dense spruce woods grow, at the end of the Viking period the forests mainly consisted of pine and birch. Spruce is a new arrival in Norwegian flora, and a thousand years ago it had not been established in Trøndelag's forests. Along the present Pilgrim's Path down the Orkla valley there was no spruce before well into the Middle Ages. Several hundred years more would pass before the dense, dark spruce wood we know well was established. The most important trees in medieval forests were birch and pine, but there were also other leafy trees than birch. Most of these are pollinated by insects, producing less pollen than the species whose pollen are spread by the wind. Studies of core samples from marshes reveal most about those species which produce much pollen.

The Virgin Mary has lent her name to many plants. The heath spotted orchid (dactylorhiza maculata) is one of the most common and also one of the most beautiful (in Norwegian called "flekkmarihand"). Photo Bjørn Sæther

Pilgrims brought their knowledge of medicinal plants. Perhaps they also brought the plants. The plant called purple gentian (gentiana purpurea) grows only along old roads in Trøndelag (in Norwegian called "søterot", i.e. sweetroot). It was used to help digestion. Photo Bjørn Sæther

Even if we do not know everything about the composition of medieval forests, we know that they must have been more open, light and less threatening than spruce woods. Today there are no more large unbroken spruce forest areas left, as this phenomenon did not last for many centuries.

The terrain through which pilgrims walked was by and large as seen today. The mountains were as steep, the rivers as wild. Valleys with their clay and gravel deposits were more narrow, woods were more open. However, there was one basic difference, that of human interference. Roads were made for riding, with minimal construction. Habitation was scarce and spread, scattered on the farms. Agriculture was more or less restricted to the sides of valleys, where the soil did not require draining systems. Forestry use was modest, as people felled a few trees for house-building, maintenance and firewood. Compared to modern cultural landscapes, the landscape seen by pilgrims must be considered virtually virginal.

Which were the nature-determined underpinnings that influenced the development of the road system in the middle ages? Along the bottom of valleys, alder trees would grow abundantly and densely, and there would be swamps and marshes in between. Rivers would meander between the hills of the valley, and large tributaries would be hard to ford, especially during periods of floods. Thus the highway would lie higher in the terrain, preferably near the divide. Steep inclines would not be such a problem when people walked or rode, but the use of wagons in the 1700s meant more attention had to be paid to the line of the road. Moreover, forests climbed higher up mountains then than now, thinning only because of climatic changes and mountain dairy farms.

A pilgrim would wander under the same heavens then as now. He would see the same mountains, and cross the same rivers. However, present-day wanderers restrict themselves to a Sunday hike, unable to gaze at the stars because of all the streetlights, and preferring a well tamed countryside before venturing into it. The pilgrim walks would be much harder, but the pilgrims were much closer to nature than we are, and mother nature would be far more present in the landscape where the pilgrims walked.

The Pilgrim City by Nidelven

by Erik Jondell

At the mouth of the Nidelven river lay the destination for the travels and wanderings of pilgrims: Nidaros (the former name of Trondheim) with Christ's Church and the shrine of the Saint King. How did Nidaros appear at the time when the influx of pilgrims reached its peak in the 1200s and 1300s? Most of the medieval city is gone now, but with the assistance of archaeologists, historians and linguists we can still draw a picture of the old Nidaros.

The history of the city is like a huge puzzle, with each new excavation yielding new information. The archaeological pieces of the puzzle, which might be buildings, streets and cemeteries from the thousand years of city history, contribute to elaborating and changing our knowledge of our past. Historical or written sources are also major pieces of the puzzle, consisting of letters and testaments, the different sagas of Kings, acts and ordinances. The city act from the early 1300s contains important information on the appearance of the city. The act describes, for example, how two teams of nightwatches were to patrol up and down the city all night to guard against the outbreak of fire. It may be assumed that approximately 3,000 people lived in the city around 700 years ago. The city lived "off the land" and the church and royal forces brought in considerable wealth through taxes and income from rent. Most was paid in goods, such as meat, corn and other agricultural produce. The income created huge profits which were used to build churches, residences and ships.

The city was not large, seen through modern eyes. The buildings were concentrated in a belt 200 to 300 meters along the river, and did not stretch further west than our Nordre gate and Munkegaten. The many small wooden houses, log-paved streets and alleys, churches and monasteries dominated the city scene. In the southern end lay the huge Christ's Church, the Archbishop's Palace and the Royal Residence. To the west there was nothing but fields and pastures, apart from the Hospital. By present-day Skansen – the redoubt – where the peninsula was at its most narrow, there was a palisade to protect the city. On the other side of the river the two monasteries Bakke and Elgeseter lay, as well as a brickworks. In the fjord there was Nidarholm monastery, and high above the city, above Steinberget, lay Sverresborg (Sverre's Castle).

The town seal of Nidaros in 1344. The motif symbolises the two powers of society – the King and the Church. The present city coat-of-arms features the same motif from the medieval city seal.

The medieval city as it may have appeared around 1300. Reconstruction sketch by Erik Jondell / Karl-Fredrik Keller

A stroll in AD 1300

Let us examine some details of the city scene more closely. Imagine entering the city as pilgrims over the long wooden bridge across the river where Elgeseter bridge lies today. Entering the peninsula, we find a watchtower, easily mistaken for a church tower. It is a steep climb from the river, and on reaching the plain, we see the large Archbishop's Palace fenced by a strong stone wall. Traffic is heavy in and out of the yard, both from the city and up from the river where the Archbishop's boats and boathouse are. We continue into the city and approach Christ's Church, but first we pass a large marble cross, recently erected by Archbishop Jørund. Nestling close to Christ's Church are many small booths where stone masons are cutting buildings blocks and beautiful sculptures. These will be placed on the west facade of the large church, now being built. Bypassing the church for the time being, we continue along the road which arches widely, turning east just north of Christ's Church. We have not yet entered the city proper where the common artisans and merchants live. Here just north of the Cathedral, we see on the left the houses of the canons.

The medieval city seen from the south as it is rendered in a model at the medieval exhibition in Vitenskaps-museet (Natural Science Museum). The route of the imaginary walk has been indicated.
Photo Vitenskapsmuseet / Roar Øhlander

We continue in the direction of the river, keeping Christ's Church and the cemetery wall on the right. Here, east of Christ's Church, lies the Royal Residence with a number of large and small buildings. The King also has his own church. By the river, almost opposite the gate of the former Royal Residence, sits the monastery of the Dominicans (no. 12 in the reconstruction on page 31). We turn north here walking down through the town, toward the fjord in the north. Now the street splits in two, and we decide to take the left branch into Langstretet (the Long Alley) for our passage through the city. This street stretches the length of the town, and it takes us all the way to the fjord. In Langstretet we pass both Allehelgenskirken (All Saints' Church) and Benediktskirken (St. Benedict's Church), and further on Gregorius' Church, and even an old stave church, St. Martin's Church. Approaching the fjord and Ørene (the sandbanks), as the area is called, houses thin out. Almost on the beach lies St. Margareta's Church with its bell tower. The tower's bells will be rung if fire breaks out in the city. Gildeskålen – the large Feasting Hall – also lies here. We turn to the right and reach the blacksmiths' booths, with soot and smoke, and the many smiths working in cramped quarters with iron and copper. There is also a mighty watch tower, similar to the one by the south bridge.

The easiest way back to Christ's Church follows the street which is parallel to the river. Down to the left by the river lies what is called Skulegården – Skule's house. This is actually the ancient royal palace which allegedly was built by Olav Tryggvason, and here lies the small Klemens Church. Immediately afterwards we enter the city again, in the busy street with all the shops – Kaupmannastretet – Merchants' Street. Now we are literally only a stone's throw from the river, where goods are being loaded and unloaded from ships by the wharves. On both sides of the street there are log buildings with shops. Between these there are small gates opening on the cobblestoned yards, with people and animals, and some pilgrims who have rented rooms in a couple of the houses. The streets are teeming with people, children playing, artisans hawking their wares and housewives hurrying past. We continue past Kaupmannastretet. On the right we have Olav's Church. People have been saying that the Franscicans will be permitted to occupy this as rumour has it that they will soon be settling here. Before we really know it, we are back by the gate of the Royal Residence again, thus also at our destination, Christ's Church.

Parts of Kaupmannastretet as uncovered at the site of the public library.

City scene from the 1200s. The crew are taking down the sails on the King's ship which is making its way upriver to moor by the wharves of the Royal Residence upriver. Langstretet is in the foreground, and on the left St. Benedict's Church is being built (where Kjøpmannsgaten 12 lies today).
Reconstruction sketch by Karl-Fredrik Keller / Øystein Ekroll

Present-day traces of the medieval city

This is perhaps the way we might imagine a tour of the city 700 years ago. But apart from the Cathedral, Erkebispegården (the Archbishop's Palace) and Vår Frue kirke (the Church of Our Lady), it is difficult to see traces of the medieval city in present day Trondheim. However, if we make an effort, we can actually find several relics of the old Nidaros in today's Trondheim. A number of today's alleys are identical to the medieval streets. Krambugata is built right on top of parts of Kaupmannastretet, Apotekerveita corresponds partly to Langstretet, and St Jørgensveita is what remains of Kirkestretet. Out of the many churches, Our Lady, the Church of Mary of the Middle Ages, is the sole surviving parish church, and traces of Gregorius' Church can be seen in the basement of Sparebanken 1 in Søndre gate. Underneath the Public Library lies Olav's Church. The Archbishop's Palace holds the impressive stone halls from the 1100s and 1200s, and parts of the old circling wall and the coin workshop are incorporated in the new museum. The medieval city may not be that obvious. But if we look carefully and are curious enough, it is obvious that modern Trondheim is built on historic ground.

Excavations have found and charted church ruins and churchyards in medieval Trondheim, but we do not know if all of them have been found. Therefore, no one is quite sure which names belong to the various church ruins. According to the most generally accepted interpretation, the names are as given below:

1. St. Margareta's Church
   (in Karl Johans gate)
2. Klemens' Church
   (underneath Trygdekontoret
   – the Social Security Building)
3. St. Martin's Church
   (under the Post Office Building)
4. Unknown church
   (St. Andrew?)
5. Gregorius' Church
   (under the Savings Bank)

6. Olav's Church, Franciscan Monastery
   (under the Public Library)
7. Church of Mary
   (Our Lady – Vår Frue kirke)
8. Korskirken
9. Allehelgenskirken – All
   Saints' Church
10. St. Benedikt's Church

11. Unknown church
    (St. Peter?)
12. Dominicans' monastery
    (under Ths. Angells Stiftelser
    – Ths. Angell's Foundations)
13. Nikolaikirken – Nikolai's Church
    in the Royal Residence
    (in the Cathedral yard)
14. Kristkirken – Christ's Church

*Photo Vitenskapsmuseet /
Roar Øhlander*

Nidaros Cathedral

by Arne Bakken

"The bells were ringing to Vespers in churches and cloisters when Kristin came into Christ's churchyard. She dared to glance for a moment up at the church's west wall – then blinded, she cast down her eyes. Human beings had never compassed this work of their own strength – God's spirit had worked in holy Øystein, and in the builders of this house that came after him."[2] – For Kristin Lavransdatter, the character in Sigrid Undset's book, Christ's Church in Nidaros was a "reflection of the glory of God's kingdom"[3]. Many have felt that the experience of beauty may produce an ethical challenge: "Now she saw how low she lay in the dust ..."[4].

Those who built the cathedral wished to create a space where heaven and earth would meet, and where pilgrims would see the greatness and the responsibility of being a human being.

Christ's Church – built on the grave of a Viking King

It was not the life Olav Haraldson lived that made him a saint, but rather his death. Through his defeat at the Battle of Stiklestad on 29 July 1030, an entire nation was eventually won over to the new faith in Christ.

Folklore about Olav tells of the profound, mysterious and life-giving relationship between impotency and power, between despair and hope, between death and life. The Cathedral brings to life the spiritual values which Saint Olav carried. The prime duty of a saint was to lead the way to Christ. His burial church was called Christ's Church in Nidaros.

A wooden chapel was built above Olav's grave immediately after he was named a saint on the 3rd of August 1031. Around AD 1070 Olav Kyrre founded the first Christ's Church in the same place. The high altar with the shrine of the King was placed where the King's grave had been.

However, the number of pilgrims rose and it was necessary to expand the church. Around AD 1150, work on the present transept was in progress. The person most thought of as the architect and builder of Nidaros Cathe-

The sculpture of Saint Olav is adorned with a wreath every St. Olav's Day, 29 July.
Photo Jøran Wærdahl

2 ibid p. 106.
3 ibid p. 106–107.
4 ibid p. 107.

Photo next page: Aune Forlag / Ole Petter Rørvik ——➤

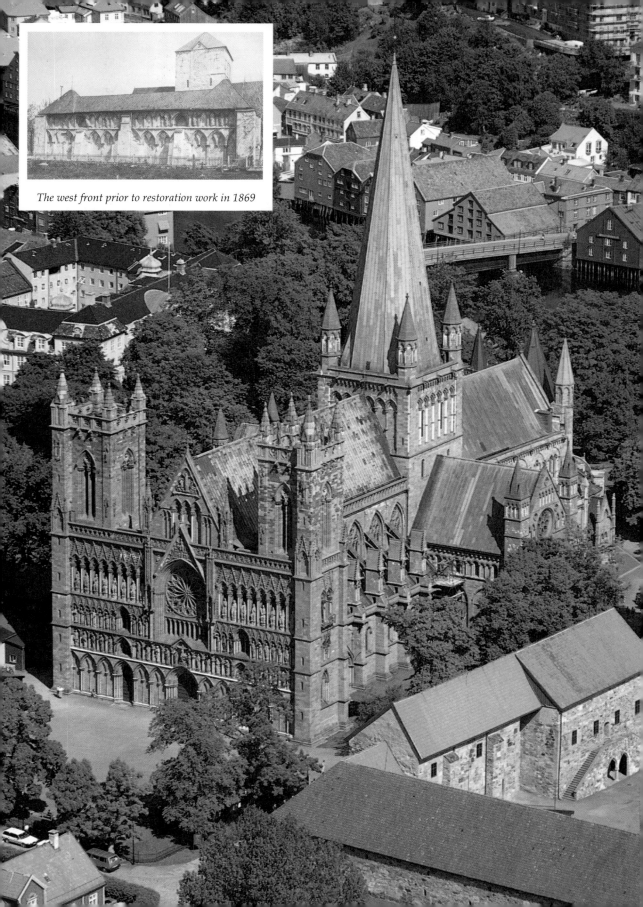

The west front prior to restoration work in 1869

Procession with relic shrine just beside the Cathedral in the 1300s. On the left one can see the arched passage between the Church and the Archbishop's Palace. Reconstruction drawing by Karl-Fredrik Keller / Øystein Ekroll

dral in its Gothic style is Øystein Erlendsson (Archbishop from 1161–1188). Born in the region, he was nevertheless a cosmopolitan, embodying European ideas and philosophies. He studied at the universities of France. On returning from his exile in England, an exile stemming from his disagreements with King Sverre, he initiated the construction of a Gothic Cathedral in 1183. Before his death he managed to finish the chapter house, and the octagon around the high altar was also started. It is generally assumed that the Cathedral in its Gothic style was finished around AD 1300.

Five times fires have ravaged the Cathedral, and five times it has been rebuilt. A major fire in 1531 ruined almost the entire west nave. When the great restoration work commenced in 1869, it was patterned on many of the places visited by Archbishop Øystein in his time. Hence, with his international outlook Øystein has become the very symbol of a Cathedral in the far North belonging to a whole family of European churches.

By visiting the Shrine of Saint Olav in Nidaros, or one of the many other Christian burial sites of saints, medieval pilgrims believed that they would be able to share in the saint's divine powers.

The Seal of Nidaros Cathedral Chapter from AD 1225 shows Saint Olav seated on his throne with a crown, lily sceptre and cross orb.

The Cathedral and the pilgrim's wanderings

In the Cathedral we can recognise the very pattern for a pilgrimage: the departure, the road, the goal – and the way home.

The west front, the entrance of the Church, constitutes a clear border where one enters a different world, thus indicating the Pilgrims' will for *departure*. The *road* is seen in the distance between the doors to the west and the *goal*, the high altar in the east. The road toward the light in the east is a wandering in the "columned wood", a wandering where the "landscape" is ever changing. There is a perception of always entering new rooms. Expectations and curiosity increase during the wandering.

At the goal, the high altar, the shrine of Saint Olav has been absent since the time of the Reformation. In the present high altar from the 1880s, the middle relief portrays the Emmaus wanderers and Christ Resurrected. The architecture with the passage around the high altar guides the pilgrims out of the church again. A pilgrim should not linger at the holy site. Part of the pilgrim journey is the *way home*. It was said about old pilgrims that they never returned to their villages without having shed at least one prejudice and replacing it with a new thought. Some times a transformation may have come about, other times not.

The Cathedral and the struggle of life

A cathedral is a spiritual common room where pilgrims find the strength to live with the tensions and contradictions within each of us.

Architecture and art, prayers and masses – all expressed the struggle of man between the light and darkness. Pain and joy, despair and hope are all placed in a larger context.

The Church is oriented in an east-west direction. The high Altar is in the east, by tradition held to be the place of Christ, the site of sunrise and the new day. Pilgrims enter from the

Birgitta from Vadstena went on a pilgrimage to Nidaros (in the 1330s), to Santiago de Compostela (1341–1343), and to Rome (1349). Her grave in Vadstena was one of the prime pilgrim shrines in the North. This sculpture of her stands on the south west front tower. Photo Jøran Wærdahl

west, where the sun goes down, the abode of darkness and life-destroying forces. The many sculptures of women and men on the west front portray people remembered because they dared to confront the darkness in all its shapes. Amongst all the holy persons we find common labourers: farmers sowing and cutting corn, women spinning and making cheese, shoemakers, blacksmiths and many others. All of them are busily engaged with the chores necessary to sustain life. Here in the Cathedral all the tasks of life are placed in a greater context. Man's day-to-day chores are part of the struggle against the forces which would destroy life!

The Cathedral reflects a continuous struggle, thus it will never really be finished while there are people on earth. This is expressed, for example, through a figure high on the west wall. We see a bricklayer with a brick in his hand and a trowel in the other. The wall behind has a empty place where the stone is to go. We and our contemporaries are also builders of cathedrals when we fight on the side of life against unfairness and the threat against life in any form. Thus the bricklayer on the west wall speaks about both the responsibility and the greatness of being human. It appears as if the Cathedral is requesting a dialogue with everyone who steps across its threshold. It appears to want something! It appears to have seen something! Cathedrals were built in a time when simply regarding things was not sufficient. The times did not distinguish between form and content, as form expressed part of the content. Therefore a person wandering in a Cathedral could not remain neutral.

Cathedral builders seem to have looked both good and evil squarely in the eye. The holy place expressed the struggle of life. In the cathedral, man was placed in the midst of the struggle between the abysses and peaks of life, with his mind and senses, his intellect and emotions, his impotence and his might.

The sculpture of the bricklayer high on the west front. Photo Jøran Wærdahl

The stonemason Josef Ankile cutting the sculpture of the apostle Jacob.
Photo Nidaros Domkirkes Restaureringsarbeider

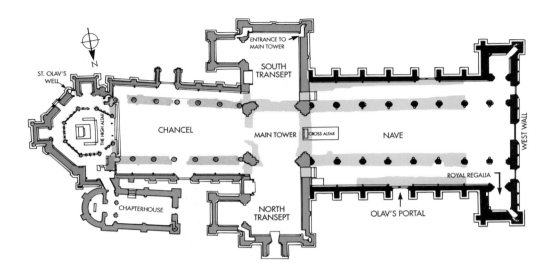

Remnants of Roman foundation wall from Olav Kyrre's church. 1066–1093.

Gothic church wall, started around 1180 by Archbishop Eystein.

Norman Roman church wall. Transept initiated in 1152 by Archbishop John, continued by Archbishop Eystein who also built the chapterhouse.

Norman Roman church wall from the first nave, commenced 1155, continued by Eystein and demolished by Archbishop Sigurd around 1230.

Gothic church wall initiated around 1230 by Archbishop Sigurd. The west front with the tower was started in 1248. Interior finished around 1320.

Up to this day, Nidaros Cathedral has been the focal point for the spiritual life of the nation. It speaks of the basic values which have been decisive for the individual and for the entire people. In one sense each person carries a cathedral within him. The pilgrim may find the inspiration in the Cathedral to discover the greatness and mystery in others and in the manifold and mysterious life of which we are all a part.

Pilgrim Badges

by Lars Andersson

Pilgrimages were an important source of revenue for the Catholic Church as pilgrims augmented collections and came bearing gifts.

This revenue was often augmented through the sale of so-called pilgrim badges. These were small decorative metal badges which were to be worn visibly, as a souvenir, as it were, a proof that a pilgrimage had been completed.

The oldest pilgrim badges in Europe are from the 12th century, but were most popular during the 14th and 15th centuries. They were mass-produced and would most often be designed as small images with a relief on one side. Being cast in an alloy of lead and tin, they would be 5–10 cm long. Since they were to be attached to the clothes, hat or bags of the wanderer, they would usually also have small loops on the sides.

A rather special form of pilgrim badges were the comb shells (*Pecten Maximus*) sold in Santiago de Compostela in north-west Spain. The shell was the icon of the apostle Jacob, and also symbolised the concept of pilgrimages.

The geographical origin of pilgrim badges is generally apparent from the design of the relief picture. It shows the purpose of the pilgrimage, the adulated saint or his/her attribute, the cult image which worked wonders or the relic. At times, the name of the place is also stated in an inscription.

The pilgrim badges from Nidaros depict Saint Olav sitting or standing with an axe in one hand and most often with a crowned orb in the other. There are a few examples of the figure being surrounded by a latticework with a round arch and small columns. None of the badges so far known have had an inscription. At present, only between ten and twenty such badges have been found, either in connection with archaeological excavations or through church restorations. However, this low number is no indication of the number of pilgrims who came to Nidaros. The finds which can be dated are from the 15th and the beginning of the 16th century, which agrees well with what we know of badges from the second great pilgrim shrine in Scandinavia, the relics of the Holy Birgitta in Vadstena. The pilgrim badges produced in

Top:
St. Olav's badge found in a triptych from the 1470s in Sånga Church in Ångermanland, Sweden. Photo Statens historiska museum, Stockholm.

Bottom:
Pilgrim shell from Santiago de Compostela, Spain, found in a grave by Västerhus chapel ruin on Frösön in Jämtland, Sweden. Photo Statens historiska museum, Stockholm

*Stoneware relic jars. Per-
haps some of them may
have been used at Olav's
well in the Cathedral.*
Photo The Science Museum /
Gorm K. Gaare

Scandinavia thus belong in the late medieval period. The places
where the badges have been found suggest that the pilgrims mainly came from the Nordic countries. So far, no Olav badges have
been found on the Continent or on the British Isles.

In addition to the traditional metal badges, we know of a special
type of miniature earthenware jar with two small handles on the
sides. Such relic jars have sometimes been used during the holy
cult in Norway. In Sweden and Denmark, however, only a few
examples of this type of jar have been found, while at least 150 jars
have been found in Norway in country houses or houses in the
small medieval towns. They have obviously had various areas of
use, but there is evidence they have been used in connection with
pilgrimages to Nidaros. Around the turn of the century, Olav's
well inside the Cathedral was cleaned. A jar was found at the bottom of the well, jammed between two stones. Perhaps a pilgrim
lost it when pouring the holy water into the jar. This holy water
and its powers was one of the reasons for the extensive pilgrimages
to Nidaros during the middle ages.

Olav Churches in Europe

by Bjørn Olav Grüner Kvam

By "Olav churches" we mean churches where St. Olav alone, or in conjunction with other saints, was used as the name or patron saint of the church when it was consecrated. From the time prior to the Reformation (before 1540, approximately), we know of at least 340 Olav churches and Olav chapels.

In Norway there have been at least 52 Olav churches. Most of those we know lie in the Oslo, Borg and Tunsberg dioceses, the northern parts of Agder diocese, Vinger, Odal and Solør deaneries in Hamar diocese, as well as Båhuslän in Sweden. In the western and northern parts of the country we find a much lower number. However, there are many churches for which we do not known who the patron saint was.

In Norway there are 17 Olav churches still standing. These are Trøgstad, Eidsberg, Ringsaker, Lom, Fiskerkapellet at Maihaugen, Sem, Våle, Borre, Hem, Tanum, Skoger Old Church, Fiskum Old Church, Bø Old Church, Seljord, Avaldsnes, Bergen Cathedral as well as Stiklestad Church. Out of these, Lom, Våle, Tanum, Avaldsnes and Bergen Cathedral usually are open in the summer. Ringsaker and Borre are travellers' churches, which also offer guided tours, refreshments and services or meditation.

Underneath Trondheim's public library you can see the remnants of an old Olav church. This church was built of stone during the middle 1100s to replace a wooden church built on the spot where the body of King Olav was kept after the Battle of Stiklestad. The stone church was the parish church until early in the 1300s, when the northernmost Franciscan monastery was founded in this place. Both the monastery and the church perished in the great city fire of 5 May 1531. The sources also mention St. Olav's Burial Chapel, probably constructed of wood, at the site where the body of Olav was moved and buried, and where the octagon in Nidaros Cathedral now stands.

In Sweden we know of at least 75 churches dedicated to St. Olav, in Denmark around 20 and in Finland at least 13. The 70 known dedications in Iceland demonstrate how strongly the Olav tradition had spread west. Olav's Church at Thingvellir is one of the most important ones, probably founded by the Saint King himself. Out of the 45 Olav churches in the British Isles, 16 still survive, four of them in London. Marygate in York, Kirkwall on the Orkneys and Waterford in Ireland are among the oldest. On the Faeroes, the Olav church at Kyrkjebø is still in use.

In the rest of Europe there were Olav chapels in Amsterdam and Maastricht in the Netherlands, and in Gdansk in Poland. In Germany and in the former Hanseatic towns St. Olav is primarily represented through altars dedicated to the Saint King, in addition to the many Olav Guilds. There are Olav altars in Bremen, Rostock and Stralsund. The Olav church in Tallin (formerly Reval), the capital of Estonia, is one of the churches still standing. The easternmost Olav church in the world is found in Novgorod (formerly Holmgard) in Russia.

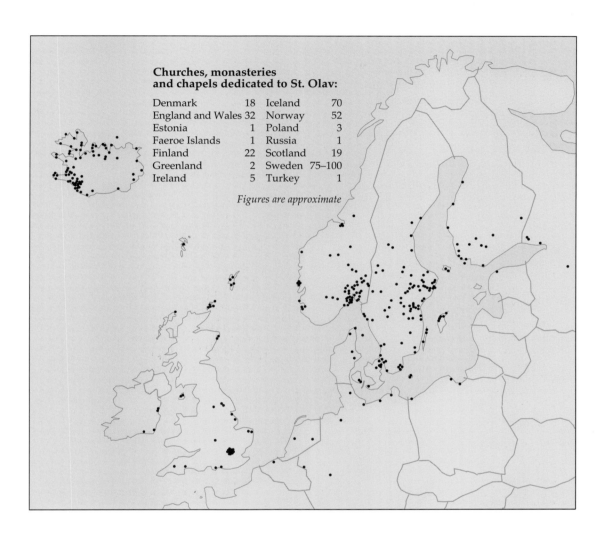

**Churches, monasteries
and chapels dedicated to St. Olav:**

Denmark	18	Iceland	70
England and Wales	32	Norway	52
Estonia	1	Poland	3
Faeroe Islands	1	Russia	1
Finland	22	Scotland	19
Greenland	2	Sweden	75–100
Ireland	5	Turkey	1

Figures are approximate

There is also an Olav church as far south as the Turkish capital of Istanbul (formerly (Miklagard/Constantinople). The occurrence of Olav churches in the Nordic countries, on the British Isles and on the Continent indicates that the Olav tradition has flourished well all over northern Europe.

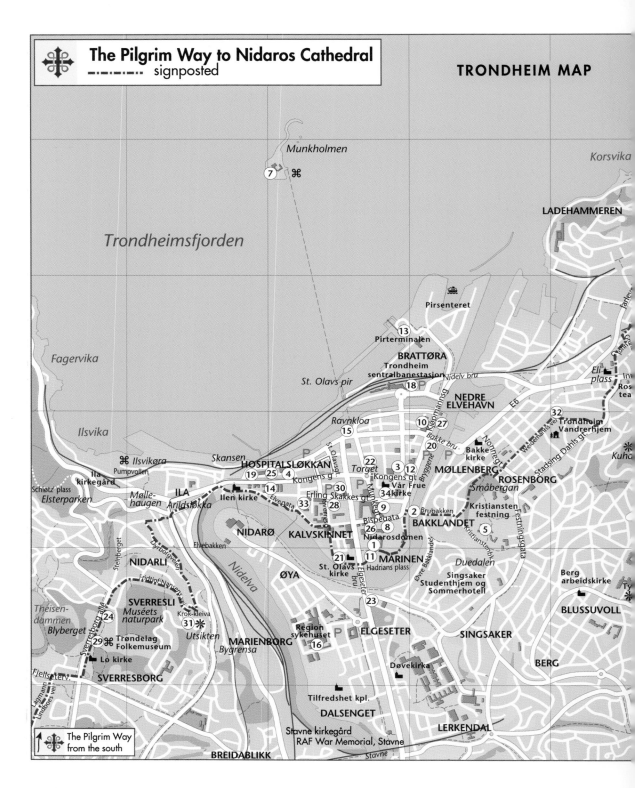

The Pilgrim Way to Nidaros Cathedral
----·--·--·---- signposted

TRONDHEIM MAP

Munkholmen

Korsvika

LADEHAMMEREN

Trondheimsfjorden

Fagervika

Pirsenteret

Pirterminalen

BRATTØRA
Trondheim
sentralbanestasjon

St. Olavs pir

Nidelv bru

Ilsvika

NEDRE
ELVEHAVN

E6

Trondheim
Vandrerhjem

Ravnkloa

Eli
plass

Int
Ros
tea

Kuho

Skansen

St. Olavsg.

HOSPITALSLØKKAN

Torget

Bakke
kirke

MØLLENBERG

Ila
kirkegård

Pumpvollen

Kongens g.

Kongens gt

Vår Frue

ROSENBORG

Ilsvikøra

Schiøtz' plass
Elsterparken

Mølle-
haugen

ILA

Arildstøkka

Ilen kirke

Elvegata

Erling Skakkes gt

34kirke

Småbergan

Kristiansten
festning

Brubakken

BAKKLANDET

Bispedata

NIDARØ

KALVSKINNET

Nidarosdomen

Duedalen

Elvebakken

ØYA

St. Olavs
kirke

MARINEN

Hadrians plass

Berg
arbeidskirke

NIDARLI

Fridtjof Nansens v.

Singsaker
Studenthjem og
Sommerhotell

BLUSSUVOLL

Theisen-
dammen
Blyberget

SVERRESLI
Muséets
naturpark

Krok-kleiva

Utsikten

Trøndelag
Folkemuseum

Region
sykehuset

MARIENBORG

Bygrensa

ELGESETER

SINGSAKER

BERG

Lo kirke

Døvekirka

SVERRESBORG

Tilfredshet kpl.

Fjellseter v.

Lindhoes vei

DALSENGET

Stavne kirkegård
RAF War Memorial, Stavne

LERKENDAL

The Pilgrim Way
from the south

BREIDABLIKK

Stavne

42

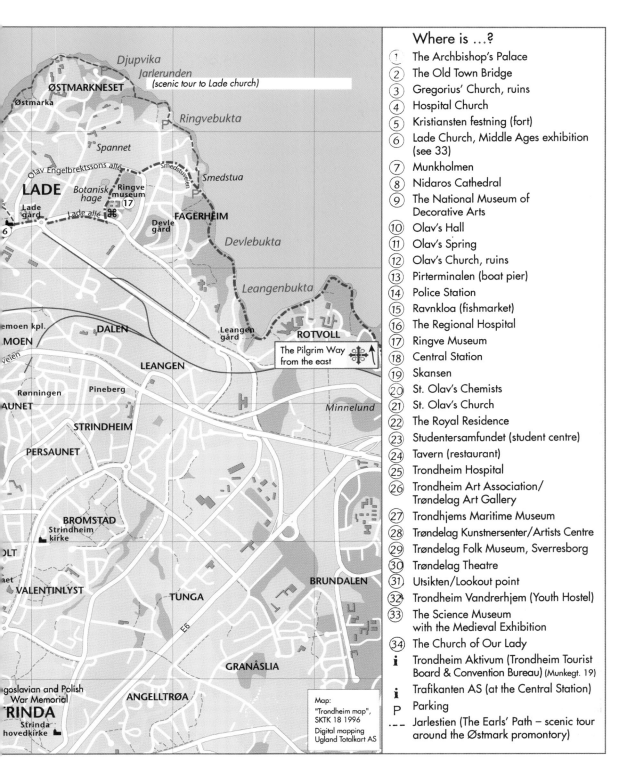

Where is ...?

1. The Archbishop's Palace
2. The Old Town Bridge
3. Gregorius' Church, ruins
4. Hospital Church
5. Kristiansten festning (fort)
6. Lade Church, Middle Ages exhibition (see 33)
7. Munkholmen
8. Nidaros Cathedral
9. The National Museum of Decorative Arts
10. Olav's Hall
11. Olav's Spring
12. Olav's Church, ruins
13. Pirterminalen (boat pier)
14. Police Station
15. Ravnkloa (fishmarket)
16. The Regional Hospital
17. Ringve Museum
18. Central Station
19. Skansen
20. St. Olav's Chemists
21. St. Olav's Church
22. The Royal Residence
23. Studentersamfundet (student centre)
24. Tavern (restaurant)
25. Trondheim Hospital
26. Trondheim Art Association/ Trøndelag Art Gallery
27. Trondhjems Maritime Museum
28. Trøndelag Kunstnersenter/Artists Centre
29. Trøndelag Folk Museum, Sverresborg
30. Trøndelag Theatre
31. Utsikten/Lookout point
32. Trondheim Vandrerhjem (Youth Hostel)
33. The Science Museum with the Medieval Exhibition
34. The Church of Our Lady

i Trondheim Aktivum (Trondheim Tourist Board & Convention Bureau) (Munkegt. 19)

i Trafikanten AS (at the Central Station)

P Parking

.-- Jarlestien (The Earls' Path – scenic tour around the Østmark promontory)

Map:
"Trondheim map",
SKTK 18 1996
Digital mapping
Ugland Totalkart AS

The Pilgrim Way
from the east

(scenic tour to Lade church)

Dear Pilgrim and Tourist

Welcome to Trondheim, the goal of your pilgrimage! We hope you'll enjoy your stay, and to help you, we're happy to provide information here about public transport, taxis, tourist information, accommodation, historic sites, museums and sights worth seeing.

Transport and tourist information

Buses and trams in the city

Most bus lines start from Munkegaten or Dronningens gate (street) in the town centre. For information on departures tel.: 73 88 44 44.

Graakallbanen (tramline) shuttles between St. Olavs gate in the centre and Lian by Bymarka, every day.

Taxi   tel.: 73 50 50 73

Outbound trains and buses

Trondheim Central Station is the joint terminal for trains and buses, and also the airport bus (flybuss) to Trondheim Airport.
Information tel.: 72 57 20 20.

Hotel booking, accommodation, guides

Trondheim Aktivum (Trondheim Tourist Board & Convention Bureau), the City Square, Munkegt. 19. Tel.: 73 92 93 94. Brochures and information about the region and the rest of the country.

Sights to see – historic sites – museums

The collection of sculptures and stones at the Cathedral

The Archbishop's Palace by Nidaros Cathedral, tel.: 73 89 08 00

The Archbishop's Palace

Scandinavia's oldest secular building. Work on it commenced during the second half of the 12th century. It was the Archbishop's residence until the Reformation. Open to visitors weekdays 12–3 (South Wing 10–5), Saturdays 12–3, Sundays 1–3.30.

The Hospital Church

Built in 1705, this is the first octagonal timber church to be built in Norway and Sweden. Situated at Trondhjems Hospital in Kongens gate. Within walking distance of the city centre.

Church ruins from the middle ages

Ruins of Olavskirken (a church from the 1100s) are found in the courtyard in the public library building at Peter Egges plass. You can see parts of the churchyard with some well-preserved skeletons. Same opening hours as the library.

In the cellar of a major savings bank you can see the ruins of Gregoriuskirken, This is a church dating back to the 1100s. It can be viewed during the bank's opening hours, at Sparebank 1 Midt-Norge, Kongens gt. 4, at the Søndre gt. (street entrance).

Munkholmen

– the Monks' Island – was the first Benedictine monastery built in the Nordic countries, built just after AD 1100. In 1658 it was converted into a prison fort. Today it is a recreational resort, with a beach and restaurant. Hourly boat departures from Ravnkloa.

Kristiansten Fort

This fort was built by General Johan Caspar de Cicignon at the time of the rebuilding of Trondheim after the 1681 fire. Memorial plaque indicates where Norwegian members of the resistance were executed during World War II. Open for admission when the fort flag is flying.

Nordenfjeldske Kunstindustrimuseum

The National Museum of Applied Art, Munkegt. 5, tel.: 73 52 13 11. Exhibitions of Norwegian and international industrial arts and design.

Olav's spring by Hadrians plass

This is the pilgrims' holy spring at the north end of Elgeseter bridge.

Ravnkloa

At the north end of Munkegaten lies Ravnkloa, the city fish market. Boats to Munkholmen.

Ringve museum

The Museum of Music History, at Lade allé 60, is the only museum in Norway with musical instruments from all over the world. There is also a lovely botanical garden here. Tel.: 73 92 24 11.

Rustkammeret / Det nordenfjeldske hjemmefrontmuseum

This is an army museum in the Archbishop's Palace, displaying uniforms and weapons. Tel.: 73 99 58 31.

Skansen

The remains of Trondheim's defences toward the west, where the city gate once stood. Today a park with a beautiful view of the fjord.

Stiftsgården

This is the largest wooden mansion in Norway, built in 1774–78 at Munkegt 23. Today it is the official Royal Residence in Trondheim. Booking for guided tours – Tel.: 73 52 13 11 / 73 52 02 58.

Gamle bybro

– the old town bridge – was first built at this site in 1681. On the west bank the old excise house still stands. The present bridge was built in 1861.

Bryggene

– the wharves – the oldest of the wharves along Nidelva river date back to the 1700s. The wharves on the seafront are from the 1800s and 1900s.

Sukkerhuset

– the Sugar Factory – at E. C. Dahls gt. 2 at Kalvskinnet, this was built as a sugar refinery in 1752, later a brewery from 1856 to 1984. This is the oldest factory building still in existence in Norway.

Trondheim Kunstmuseum / Trøndelag Kunstgalleri

– the art gallery – Bispegt. 7B. Situated across from Nidaros Cathedral, the Art Gallery has a large collection of art from Norway and other countries from about 1800 and up to modern times. Tel.: 73 52 66 71 or 73 52 37 45.

Trondhjems Hospital

At Hospitalsløkkan 2–4, this is the oldest existing social institution in Norway, founded in 1277 as a place to nurse lepers and poor people, and also served as a pilgrim hospice. Now used as a home for the elderly.

Trøndelag Folkemuseum, Sverresborg

The Folk Museum is the central museum for cultural history in the region. Located on the site of King Sverre's 800-year-old castle, his mount Zion, 60 buildings have been placed here and restored, including a stave church, mountain farms, boathouses, city houses and manors. The Trøndelag Ski Museum is also located here. Booking of guided tours tel.: 73 89 01 00. Tavern, an inn from 1739, is open all year, tel.: 73 52 09 32.

Trøndelag kunstnersenter

Trøndelag artists' centre – Sverres gt. 7. Tel.: 73 52 49 10. Contemporary art.

Vitenskapsmuseet (Natural Science Museum). Erling Skakkes gt. 47 B.

The science museum presents Norwegian nature and cultural history, including mammals, birds, insects fish and marine animals from Norway and beyond. The cultural history section displays medieval church adornments, saints, crucifixes, altar pieces and pulpits beautifully carved in wood.

The Medieval Exhibition

(at Vitenskapsmuseet) displays finds from the city grounds, and a recreated city section with streets and houses. The picture show entitled *Byen under gaten* – the City underneath the Streets – offers fascinating glimpses into medieval Trondheim. Open Tuesday–Friday 10–5, Saturday and Sunday 11–5.

Medieval Churches

Byneset church, originally Mikaelskirken at Stein from 1170–80, Spongdal at Byneset. A pagan place of worship during pre-Christian times was close to where the church now stands. Tel.: 72 83 58 40.

Lade church from around 1180, Lade allé 36. There was a pagan place of worship 100 hundred meters north-east of Lade farm during pre-Christian times.

The Church of Our Lady (Vår Frue kirke) was originally Mariakirken from the 1200s. Kongens gt. 5 on the south end of Nordre gate.

Nidaros Cathedral

Services at 11 and 6 on Sundays. Prayer meeting at 12.15 Mondays–Saturdays. Organ recital weekdays and each Saturday at 1. During the tourist season evening service for all travellers every day at 5.45. Regular guided tours in Norwegian, English, German and French at 11, 2, and 4 Monday–Friday. Admission to the Cathedral tower every 30 minutes.

Crown regalia on display Monday–Friday 9–6.15 and Sunday 1–4. Evening prayer in the chapterhouse each Friday at 8 PM. Music service each Saturday at 1.

The Catholic Church in Trondheim

St. Olavs kirke (originally from 1872), Schirmers gt. 1. Open for prayers 8–7. Sundays: Early mass at 9. High mass at 11.

Trondheim – a town of culture

The Olav's Festival in Trondheim
– *Olavsfestdagene*

This church and culture festival is based upon St Olav's Day and Nidaros Cathedral, taking place at the end of July and lasting into the first week of August.

St Olav's day marks the death of Saint Olav at the Battle of Stiklestad. Since medieval times this has been an important celebration, both as a tradition within the church and for the people. Nidaros Cathedral is the religious focus during the celebration. Now pilgrims are returning to Nidaros, some walking the Pilgrim Path, some by modern means of transport. During the last days of July there are small and larger services in a number of the city churches. The major event is "Olavsvaka" – Olav's Wake in the Cathedral, during the night between 28 and 29 July.

The cultural events during the celebration of St Olav include concerts, theatrical performances, lectures, exhibitions, pilgrim wanderings and excursions. The celebration of the people has found its expression in a historical market where the mood and commotion of medieval fairs is recreated, with sales of the work of artisans, demonstrations of old handicraft techniques, refreshments and entertainment. The *Olavsfestdagene* office is situated at Dronningens gt. 1B. Tel.: 73 92 94 70. Fax: 73 50 38 66.

Olavshallen – the concert hall

Concerts all year round in the two concert halls at Kjøpmannsgt. 44. Tickets and information tel.: 73 99 40 50.

Trondheim Symphony Orchestra

Concerts every week. Tickets and information, tel.: 73 53 98 00. Season programme can be obtained in the ticket booth at Olavshallen, Kjøpmanns gt. 44.

Trøndelag Theatre

Prinsens gt. 18–20. Tickets and information, tel.: 73 80 50 00.

Good to know

Trondheim Folkebibliotek – Trondheim Public Library

Peter Egges pl. 1. Tel.: 72 54 75 20 and 72 54 75 00. During the summer season open Mondays—Fridays 9–4, Saturdays 9–2.

Post Office

The main post office is at Dronningens gt. 10. Tel.: 73 95 84 00.

Open Mondays–Fridays 8–5, Thursday 8–6. Saturdays 9–2. Mail to be called for. Stamp shop.

Police Station

Kongens gt. 87. Tel.: 73 89 90 90.

Medical emergencies:
Casualty hospital tel.: 73 52 25 00
Dental emergencies tel.: 73 50 55 00

Chemist Emergency Service: St. Olav apotek, Kjøpmannsgaten 65 by Bakke bridge. Opening hours: weekdays 8.30–Midnight, Sundays 10–Midnight. Tel.: 73 52 66 66.

Emergency:
Police: 112
Fire: 110
Ambulance: 113

Municipality of Trondheim, administration: City Hall, Munkegata 1, by Nidaros Cathedral. Tel.: 72 54 65 02, fax: 72 54 60 64.

Inhabitants: 144,670 (1 January 1997)

Residential units: approximately 61,000

Area: 342 km^2

A Brief History of Trondheim

by Jon Øyvind Eriksen

Trondheim was founded in 997 by Olav Tryggvason. However, houses had been built by the mouth of Nidelven – the river Nid – much earlier than this. After the Battle of Stiklestad in 1030, when the body of Saint Olav was taken to Trondheim, the town grew in importance. In the same year, the town was made the capital of Norway, and Nidaros Cathedral eventually became one of the major pilgrim shrines in Europe. In 1152 the town was made the seat of the Archbishop, and the Archbishop's Palace became the centre of power in a realm stretching from Norway to Greenland. The Black Death caused a major setback for the town, but it really declined in importance when the Danish King introduced the Reformation. In 1537 the last Archbishop in Nidaros, Olav Engelbrektsson, fled the country.

During the following centuries, the town suffered through hardships. After the Peace Treaty of Roskilde in 1658, Trondheim fell into Swedish hands, but it was re-conquered just seven months later. In 1681, the whole town burned to the ground. The King commanded General Major Johan Caspar de Cicignon to design a completely new plan for the city which can still be observed in today's downtown street plan. At the same time, Kristiansten fort was also built. During the Great Nordic War, not many years later, this fort saved the city from being conquered by a Swedish army under the command of General Armfelt. During their retreat, 3,000 Swedish soldiers perished in a snowstorm in the border mountains. During the same war naval hero Peter Wessel Tordenskjold from Trondheim established himself as one of the most famous admirals of the Danish-Norwegian fleet.

Financial development in the 1700s was led by rich merchants who traded in exports and imports using their own ships. The greatest of them all, Thomas Angell, left his fortune to the city poor. However, city authorities spent portions of this money on other deserving projects, including the first city waterworks constructed in 1777. The rich merchants usually lived along Kjøpmannsgaten, with their wharves facing the river. These are still a characteristic feature of the city today. The great wooden mansions in the city, the Royal Residence probably being the most well-known, were built during this time of prosperity.

Industrialisation in the 1800s led to new growth for the city. A number of factories and workshops were founded, and Trondheim was connected by railway to the south. The railway via Røros was opened in 1877, and the one across the Dovre mountains in 1921.

At the end of the 1800s, Trondheim also developed into a centre for education. *Trondhjems tekniske Læreanstalt* (Technical Institute) was founded in 1870, and *Norges tekniske Høgskole*, NTH, (The Norwegian Institute of Technology) was established in 1910. Twelve years later *Norges lærerhøgskole*, NLHT, (The Norwegian College of Education) was founded, and in 1968 Stortinget (the Norwegian Parliament) decided to establish the University of Trondheim comprising NTH, NLHT and Vitenskapsmuseet (Det Kongelige Norske Videnskabers Selskab – The Royal Norwegian Scientific Society). In 1996, all the units of the university were merged into *Norges teknisk-naturvitenskapelige universitet* (NTNU) – the Norwegian University of Science and Technology.

The status of the city as a centre of administration and education led to a rise in population. In 1964, the neighbouring municipalities of Strinda, Tiller, Leinstrand and Byneset were merged with Trondheim. A number of suburbs sprung up. Trondheim was an industrial city for a long time, but its role as a city of knowledge and research has gained increasing importance. Today the city has the second largest university in Norway, NTNU, and SINTEF, the renowned research foundation. In its role as an administrative centre and a city of culture, Trondheim plays an important role for the whole region of *Midt-Norge* – central Norway.

Literature for pilgrims

Almaas, Mads: *Gamle ferdselsveier.* [Old highways] Spor – fortidsnytt fra Midt-Norge, no. 1/1988

Anderson Lars: *Pilgrimsmärken och vallfart* [Pilgrim badges and pilgrimages].
Almquist & Wiksell International 1989.

Bakken, Arne: *Pilgrimsvandring før og nå* [Pilgrimages before and now]
Nidaros Domkirkes restaureringsarbeiders forlag, 1992. Småskriftserie no. 10.

Bakken, Arne: *Nidarosdomen – en pilegrimsvandring* [Nidaros Cathedral – a pilgrim's tour].
Aschehoug forlag, 1997.

Blom, Grethe Authén: *Nidaros som pilgrimsby* [Nidaros as a pilgrim's city].
Nidaros Domkirkes restaureringsarbeiders forlag, 1994. Småskriftserie no. 6

Blom, Grethe Authén: *Helgenkonge og helgenskrin* [A saintly King and a saint's shrine].
Nidaros Domkirkes restaureringsarbeiders forlag, 1994. Småskriftserie no. 9

Bratberg, Terje: *Trondheim Byleksikon* [The Encyclopaedia of Trondheim City]. Kunnskapsforlaget, 1997.

Bremen, Adam: *Beretningen om Hamburgs stift* [The Account of Hamburg Diocese].
Thorleif Dahls kulturbibliotek, Aschehoug forlag, 1993.

Christophersen, Axel: *Landet byen bygde* [The country built by the city]. Spor – fortidsnytt fra Midt-Norge, no. 2/1989.

Christophersen, Axel: *Folk og bebyggelse i Middelalderens Trondheim* [People and buildings in medieval Trondheim].
Spor – fortidsnytt fra Midt-Norge, no. 2/1992.

Dahlin, Elin: *Bygghytten ved Nidarosdomen* [The builders' hut by Nidaros Cathedral]
Spor – fortidsnytt fra Midt-Norge, no. 2/1987.

Dahlin, Elin: *Fem år etter brannen* [Five Years after the Fire]. Spor no. 2/1988.

Dahlin, Elin: *Gipsmakere ved Nidarosdomen* [Plasterers by Nidaros Cathedral]. Spor, no. 1/1990.

Det Norske Samlaget: *Passio Olavi: Lidingssoga og undergjerningane åt den heilage Olav* [Passio Olavi: The saga of sufferings and the wonders worked by Saint Olav].
Translation from the Latin by Eilif Skard, 1995.

Ekroll, Øystein et al.: *Nidaros Domkirke og erkebispegården* [Nidaros Cathedral and the Archbishop's Palace].
Nidaros Domkirkes restaureringsarbeiders forlag, 1995.

Grankvist, Rolf: *Nidaros kirkes spital 700 år – Trondhjems Hospital 1277–1977* [Nidaros Cathedral's Hospital 700 years – Trondhjems Hospital 1277–1977]. F. Bruns Bokhandels forlag, 1982.

Gustafson, Lill: *Farlig ferd i fjellet* [Dangerous journey in the mountains]. Spor – fortidsnytt fra Midt-Norge.

Jones, Michael: *Kulturlandskapet* [The culture landscape]. Spor – fortidsnytt fra Midt-Norge, no. 2/1989.

Kollandsrud, Mari: *Pilgrimsleden til Nidaros* [The Pilgrim Way to Nidaros].
Riksantikvaren, Gyldendal Norsk Forlag, 1997.

Langslet, Lars Roar: *Olav den Hellige* [Saint Olav]. Gyldendal Norsk Forlag, 1995.

Luthen, Eivind: *I pilegrimenes fotspor* [Following the footsteps of the Pilgrims]. Cappelen, 1992.

Luthen, Eivind: *På pilegrimsferd* [On a Pilgrimage]. Pilegrimsforlaget, 1995.

Selnes, Arnulf: *Vandring langs gamle veifar* [Wandering along Old Roads]. Tapir, 1995.

Smedstad, Ingrid: *Veier i myr* [Marsh roads]. Spor – fortidsnytt fra Midt-Norge no. 1/1988.

Weber, Birthe: *I pilegrimenes spor* [On the path of the pilgrims].
Spor – fortidsnytt fra Midt-Norge no. 1/1988.

Eds.: *Trondheims historie 1–6* [The History of Trondheim 1–6, Universitetsforlaget 1997.]
Jørn Sandnes   Vol. 1: Grethe Authén Blom: *Hellig Olavs by. Middelalderen til 1537*
Rolf Grankvist   [The City of Olav the Saint. The Middle Ages until 1537].
Anders Kirkhusmo   Vol. 2: Steinar Suphellen: *Innvandrernes by. 1537–1800* [The City of Immigrants. 1537–1800].

Vol. 3: Knut Mykland: *Fra Søgaden til Strandgaden. 1800–1880*
[From Søgaden to Strandgaden. 1800–1880].

Vol. 4: Rolf Danielsen: *En exempelløs fremgang. 1880–1920*
[Progress without Compare. 1880–1920].

Vol. 5: Anders Kirkhusmo: *Vekst gjennom krise og krig. 1920–1964*
[Growth through Crisis and War. 1920–1964].

Vol. 6: Ola Svein Stugu: *Kunnskapsbyen. 1964–1997* [The City of Knowledge. 1964–1997].

Natur, kultur og tro i middelalderen [Nature, culture and beliefs during the Middle Ages].
The Directorate for Nature Management and the Directorate for Cultural Heritage, 1997.